I hope you enjoy!

Crystal Poems: Vol. 1

Ruby…

So many people seem 2 want a war.
Courage won't come from hearts that aren't prepared.
Ruby in thy breast, beneath what is layered
With love helps explain what one's fighting for.

Certain veins salute liquified Ruby.
Blood infused with it flow as the Red Sea.
Roars from the lions sound like a medley
While the crystal inspires soldiers 2 be.

Struggling for better is always good.
Being a person known as a fixer
Relieves hearts devoid of an elixir
That helps the warrior pump special blood ❤

Onyx...

Ethiopian nights where hyenas roam
& work with lions deep in the dark cover
Host a crystal seeming in love with its home
So much that it helps join u with your lover.

Onyx is one that strikes 2 protect your heart
As if 2 help peace of mind become normal.
Strong response delights akin 2 works of art
As bearers pioneer in what is formal.

Sophisticated crystals like Onyx move
Unwanted notions away excessively.
This stone sparks awareness & helps behoove
Us 2 consider its use expressively ✿

Emerald...

She's for strong wills that love adventure,
Juicy words & passionate heat,
Soulful emotions that lead 2 real life
& may surprise with heavy delight.

Her name is Emerald, that's for sure!
She will not get used 2 defeat.
Her power is sharp & cuts like a knife
If one dare challenge her 2 a fight ❀

Gold...

Time will tell just how valuable it is.
Mysteries may be uncovered if it's seen.
Some look forward 2 the Hereafter for this
& in this life, drape it perfectly with green.

Time will tell just how valuable it is.
Love may be expressed by using its impact.
It may be for her body & not for his
But he enjoys how their connection's exact.

Time will tell just how valuable it is ✨

Amethyst (pt. 1)…

Imagine –

Majestic structures began 2 emerge
Boldly as kings walking there in the sun.
Erections fashion an energy surge,
Becoming Amethyst when they are done.
Signals regulate rhythm with merit,
Leaving formulas we can inherit..

Crowns would miss much without it.

END OF PART ONE

Lapis Lazuli...

They say the best blue Lapis comes from Afghan,
Nestled in mountains, maybe near Kush.
Places in this region have produced for man
Strains of plants including a small bush
That elevate senses & we feel a rush
Of psychedelic effects inside.
Lapis Lazuli looks like an ocean's tide
Raging across Pyrite as its sand.
Clouds of white Calcite excite the lucky hand
That holds this gorgeous blue crystal ride.
Mysterious Lapis found in stories told
Moons long ago are still beautiful!
It demands your attention & u will mull
At its grandeur as stories of old ❧

Carnelian (Aqeeq)...

Carnelian warmth, encased in a tomb
Puzzles top excavators & pirates.
Fire is calm as a child in a womb
As long as it's inside of thy breastplates.

Pyramids channel its energy force
& become empowered for those who use.
The Prophet wore it, according 2 source,
With wisdom while it may help others muse.

May peace be upon all of our Prophets.

Rituals increase as understanding
Of nature becomes honestly clearer.
Posture strengthens & seem so commanding
When Carnelian anchors its bearer.

Pure Sufi wisdom amidst crystal cures
May open a world of great benefit.
Carnelian stone easily ensures
Users with what it has inside of it ❦

Opal...

She's so sweet if u love her well.
If u mistreat love, she'll be firm.
Sacred emotions hurl a spell
On those who cheat & breach their term ✻

Libyan Desert Glass...

Interesting travels begin 2 pursue
Like winds across the cool desert sands.
Moonlit creatures look forward 2 skies anew.
Scarab Beetles work hard with their hands.
The area where this desert glass is found
May even surprise expert seekers.
Calling for what deepest intrigues will surround,
Brave miners search for this stone's features.
In olden times, its uses were magical
Maybe for reasons unknown today
Or maybe its uses are so practical
That space warps happen without delay.
Libyan Desert Glass is such a crystal
& it remains as one mystical ✨

Shungite...

Russian Carbon found 2 be of use
By those who welcome what they attract.
It protects from microwave abuse
& helps clean water upon contact.

Spirit Quartz...

Interesting name..
This crystal has an interesting name!
I walked in a gem show & all of a sudden,
I feel something pulling me.
It felt like a magnet
Or a child 2 a mother.
It was communication at its finest.
I could not part from it.
Telepathy from a distance
Without a resistance
In that instance
Was magnificent
South African vibrations..
Frequencies, stations 🐦

Amethyst (pt. 2)…

Imagine –

Deep purple blood satiates her light body.
She swims underwater ready 2 love.
Mermaids & queens may have the same hobby,
Collecting Amethyst while on the move.
Audiences embrace the notation
Of this purple stone's orientation.

Knights & supporters prepare for battle.
They mustn't return lest victory's won.
Before they load up horses & saddle,
Courageous moods overtook everyone.
Their desires are moved by Amethyst
Placed in braided leather hilts in their fist.

Some believe good fortune may soon follow
& hearts may fix when royalty can rest.
Knowing peace prepares us for the morrow,
Chants & oaths shouted from those who confessed
That honor & glory are so precious.
They pledged what became very infectious.

Numbers increase & now the march begins.
Songs by mermaids are irresistible.
Melodies clean water pushed by their fins
& majestic structures are visual.
Crown crystals are used at various times
Of interaction, shifting paradigms.

Adjustments are effortless with this stone.
Her Crown is delighted once she sees it.
The crystal glistens atop of her throne
& fragrance surrounds all that she sees fit.
Her humble abode smells of Purple Mist,
Existing in nostrils that fortune kissed.

Mermaids can interpret the queen's motives.
Often, they relate in different ways.
Selecting a crystal that helps growth gives
Reason 2 many as they approach days.
Most of her court can't understand her plight.
Regularly, she expresses her might.

A citing for magic may bring trouble
Yet, strangers in all of her rooms scare youth.
Some saw dolls move their feet in a shuffle
By the queen's "Selfie Art Portal" or booth
Before green lace fell off of a mirror
Into hands of nobody seen near her.

Their queen wants Amethyst found in water.
She sends knights out on quests every year.
Some people know fire can get hotter
If Her Majesty persists & they fear
Unsuccessful results they've seen before.
It made Her Highness let out a loud roar

So earthquakes may warn & strong winds may blow
& rivers may run an unusual course
Before these knights ignore what may bestow
Them from The Crown & what it does indorse.
The order of conduct is uniform
In order 2 trust when there is a storm.

They move toward the ocean near distant lands
Where women in scarves made of silk sip tea.
Sufi warriors will lend helping hands.
They seem 2 know the mermaids in the sea.
Knights approach this year with small Amethyst
Included in white bracelets on their wrist

Which was a peace sign 2 the warriors
Who show similitude & supreme grasp.
Connections 2 the sea thru corridors
Help this Amethyst remain in their clasp
& sometimes, warriors may disappear
In secret portals though they seem austere.

Bad luck may befall he who disrespects
Their constant reminders that nature give.
Usually, the poor victim detects
The seizure too late 2 be calmative.
Knights understand their mission for the queen
& begin 2 intercede in this scene ❀

END OF PART TWO

Zircon...

The balance that Zircon helps bring unlocks
An appreciation held within hearts.
Needless 2 say, some love the direction.
Usually, they have beautiful starts
2 their courses & like determined darts,
Their skill strengthens as they cut thru the rocks
Akin 2 wind when they need protection.
Zircon's sure 2 be in the selection.

Topaz...

The moon & sun has reasons 2 exist.
Some stones are formed under their rotations,
Capturing what a few dare not resist
While lifting veils that hide one's notations.

Electric charges may help u beware
Of Topaz influence & how it's used.
Psychic clarity levels become rare,
Seen by a few because others refused.

Amber...

Stuck in a fossilized form, the gnat remains.
Amber guarded its body for many years.
It seems 2 capture inner-electric fears
& put them away along with other pains.

Beautiful resin crystallized & golden
Work well with other stones within our chamber.
The Amber smoke repels chaos & danger.
It reinvigorates what once was olden ☀

Lemurian Seed Crystals…

Love can open doors needed for safety.
Patience uncovers a world of benefit.
Gratitude awakens what darkness unlit
As we gather these crystals faithfully.

Some people approach us with wondrous eyes
& ask about steps we see with this stone.
Seed Crystals were found resting alone.
Perhaps information can come from the skies.

Worlds beyond this one exist without doubt!
Knowledge has come in most vivid detail
About advancement 2 those who don't fail
At sharing love as they move about.

Lemurian Crystals are easy 2 use.
Labyrinths filled with amazing luck
Seem 2 surprise onlookers who are stuck
While users navigate as they choose.

Sleeping beside Crystals may help u feel sane.
We hope your dreams are good & pure.
Learn how 2 discern between obscure
& clear with this one again & again ❦

Black Tourmaline...

Imagine –

It grows from a matrix toward rays of the sun,
Protecting lasers from entering rooms.
Its tight vigor decodes distant depressions,
Synchronizing wish with the opposite.

Impeccable defense (second 2 none)
Is how it stands confidently against glooms,
Persists & allows u 2 keep lessons
Safe as a chest with locks on top of it.

Cool Black Tourmaline.

Rose Quartz...

Soft fragrances endow the fortunate.
Auras surrounded with sensuous pink
Rose colors, beautiful & pleasing 2 the touch
Raise your insight so it does not sink.
Crystals enhanced with pink interior
Seem 2 easily soothe a broken spirit.
A gentleman feels that he'll always be here for her,
Saying a sweet word so she can hear it.
Love Stone Holders may appear
& aren't afraid 2 treat people right.
Principles rooted in love & fear
Of loosing gifts we hold so dear
Help us win in every fight
& help us sleep well thru the night ✿

Hematite…

Remembering memories while balancing scales
Make way for advancements into the Next Life.
Solid ground allows us 2 move like whales
With confidence akin 2 wind behind ship sails
Or Hematite Holders removed from strife.

Precise manifestations open an ocean.
Magnetic energy brought out by the stone
May harness what wizards would like in a potion,
Put that which is beneficial in motion,
& still remain socially left alone.

Labradorite...

Some dimensions may open gates
That avert most from ousting fears
While Labradorite instigates
Fancies 2 move as if on skates
Thru levels not seen by most peers.

Diamond…

Exciting mirrors show light in colors,
Strengthening relationships once broken.
Magical reflections shine towards others,
Keeping the arms of good friends wide open.

Diamonds are examples of such powers,
Amplifying life thru energy spells.
Holders may feel how their aura towers,
Helping some merchants make easier sells ✿

Tibetan Tektite...

Dark space evidence may've lit the sky red
As molten rock falls from the skies above
But these bits are found cool & black instead.
They seem 2 serve as signs for protected
Areas that most have no knowledge of.

Extraterrestrial & used on Earth,
The lightweight stones may feel strange 2 your touch.
Your first elevation may welcome birth
2 new ideas that point towards its worth,
Giving reason 2 why some use it much.

Tektites are not always recommended.
Careful use is standard encouragement.
Outcomes may not be what you've intended
Due 2 words u wish could be rescinded
But have patience, for its like nourishment ⊛

Jade...

Dreams may show a fortune.
Gifts come in many ways.
Jade Holders want more soon.
It sure helps brighten days.

Danburite...

Spiritual dreams are often misunderstood.
Anxiety may occur & frighten us.
Awakenings 2 new lives bring about fuss
From uneasy mental states we don't discuss.

If someone would introduce them 2 this, thus
Activating higher consciousness for good,
Maybe families stay in their neighborhood
& spread wisdom 2 those standing where they stood.

Crystallized Wood…

What has it experienced?
Rings inside may hold stories.
Patience could show us a truth.
It's something about old wood.
Masked at first & then we sensed
Inner-peace without worries
Of death akin 2 our youth,
Standing as the old tree stood ❧

Turquoise…

Lightning usually avoids the keeper.
Skies make way for benefits 2 reach us.
Turquoise Holders have a lot 2 teach, thus
Strengthening those who're otherwise weaker.

Clear Quartz Crystal…

& what can I tell u of Clear Quartz Crystal?
It leans toward perfection, undoubtedly!
Magnified simplicity has made it mystical
2 those who're unsure of what it's made out 2 be.

This gift may amplify cognizant minds
& help those 2 focus when staring at a sphere.
Looking into the ball is not for future finds
But 2 see in one's mind what images appear.

Many of these practices are misunderstood.
Some are left out due 2 wisdom & duty.
Keeping lucid thoughts is always good
As long as one's heart is in a state of beauty.

Clear Quartz Crystal can help verities unfold.
Traveling's easier when clarity rests.
Treasures inside your chamber behold
What others forsake 2 have in their breasts.

Palpable arrangements that include this stone
May welcome its ability 2 kindle data.
Those who experiment are amazed at what's shone,
For Clear Quartz Crystal completes their schemata ☕

Amethyst (pt. 3)…

Imagine an impressive purple stone
That's powerful 2 those who see its glare.
This kind can be carried with u alone
& used for comfort as long as u stare.
All stones have a purpose for being here.
Some are dear simply for how they appear.
Elders spoke about these Purple Crystals
& decorated kings who praise their queen.
Some use these crystals for their rituals.
Maybe they would make love in a routine
Or wage war against all the world below
& watch it burn as if they were Nero
But Amethyst makes her a happy queen
& some systems aren't meant 2 come between 🐦

END OF PART THREE

Moldavite...

Green Mystery is upheld beyond the artificial.
Its nexus between literal & abstract vibrations
Hit frequencies that are noticed easily
& spellbinds the holder right from the initial
Contact, seeing tunnels thru its striations.
Sometimes, things are what they seem 2 be.
Face this crystal toward the sky 2 glow.
Space travel is facile & how pretty is the Milky Way?!
It helps 2 have gratitude & unlock the heart.
Cryptic Moldavite may help us grow.
Its green influence aid with the day.
Once familiar, you'll not want 2 part.
Emotions intensify & compassion accelerates,
Bringing clarity 2 thee who meditates 🐣

BONUS

Eclipse Poem…

Sunlit precious love
Moves all around us.
Clouds congest above
As all members wait.
Know what 2 think of
Now & later, thus
Open a new gate.
Once u enter rooms,
Spread love all around.
Show them what you've found.
Take away their gloom.
An eclipse is here,
A solar eclipse!
Love is all around!

(Written while a solar eclipse was in: 8/21/2017 Nashville, TN)

THANK YOU!

Made in the USA
Lexington, KY
15 February 2018